D1451709

SHOW-ME-HOW
I Can Have a Party!

Simple-to-make party ideas
for young children

THOMASINA SMITH

SMITHMARK

First published in 1996 by
SMITHMARK Publishers,
a division of US Media Holdings Inc.,
16 East 32nd Street,
New York, NY 10016

SMITHMARK books are available for bulk purchase
for sales promotion and premium use. For details
write or call the manager of special sales,
SMITHMARK Publishers, 16 East 32nd Street
New York, NY 10016: (212) 532 6600.

Produced by Anness Publishing Limited
1 Boundary Row
London SE1 8HP

ISBN 0-8317-5676-4

Publisher: Joanna Lorenz
Senior Editor, Children's Books: Sue Grabham
Assistant Editor: Sophie Warne
Photographer: John Freeman
Designer: Edward Kinsey

Printed and bound in China

PLEASE NOTE
**The level of adult supervision needed will
depend on the age and ability of the children
following the projects. However, we advise that
adult supervision is always vital when the project calls for the use of sharp knives or other
utensils. Always keep potentially harmful tools
well out of the reach of young children.**

Contents

Introduction

This book is full of great ideas for making your party extra special. The step-by-step projects cover all the ingredients of a good party: games, decorations, food and costumes.

Some of the ideas in this book follow a theme. If you are excited by a particular theme you can make it the focal point of your party. Some of the themes included in this book are jungle, desert island, funfair and Halloween.

You can have as much fun preparing for a party as during it.

Treasure chests are good places to hide presents in.

Protect your clothes if you are going to do something messy.

When Making Things

1 Try to leave yourself plenty of time before the party.
2 Read through the instructions carefully.
3 Make a list of all the materials and tools you will need. You may need the help of someone older than you for finding or buying materials or tools.
4 Prepare your work space. Cover the surface you are working on, in case you spill anything. Make sure you have enough room.
5 Put on a smock or apron to protect your clothes, or wear old clothes that are already stained.
6 When cooking, wash your hands thoroughly.
7 Always clean up as you go along. Make sure anything that might spill is in a safe place.
8 At the end of a project thoroughly wash brushes in lukewarm water with a little detergent. Put lids on paints. Wipe surfaces.
9 Be extra careful with sharp tools, scissors or knives. Always make sure sharp instruments are pointing down, away from your face. If you need help, ask someone older.
10 If you're not sure what to do, always ask a grown-up for help.

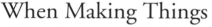

Cover your work surface with newspaper or plastic.

Crocodile tunnels are fun to crawl through.

Handy Techniques for Difficult Projects

Here are some handy tips for projects that require extra attention.

Cutting Out a Circle Using Scissors

The best method if you do not need the circle cut-out is to draw your circle, then cut into the center of the circle first. Cut lines from the center to the edge, so that the circle is divided into segments. Then cut around the edge of the circle. Cutting off the segments will leave you with a neater edge.

Painting Straight Lines

If you find painting a straight line difficult, use masking tape to mark just above or below where you want the line. Paint your line, and leave it to dry. When you remove the masking tape (carefully) the line will be straight and even.

If you need to use scissors or a knife, ask an adult for help.

Painting Round Objects

It helps when painting a curved object, such as an egg or a ball, to rest it in a holder. That way it won't roll around

Masking tape can help you paint a straight line.

You can decorate a cake to match the theme of your party.

when it is drying. Plastic bowls, mugs and egg boxes make excellent holders.

A mixture of glue and water can be painted over the surface of paint. This makes the surface waterproof and protects it. The mixture is see-through when it has dried.

Round objects are easier to paint when they are propped up.

Templates and Guides

Some of the projects in this book have templates for you to use. There are also guides for some other projects showing you the correct measurements to follow.

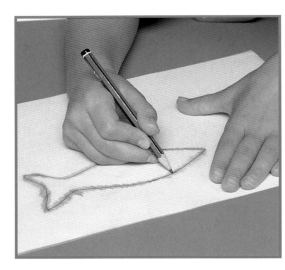

1 Place a piece of tracing paper over the template in the book. Holding the paper still, trace the pattern using a soft pencil. Turn the tracing paper over and scribble over the outline with your pencil.

2 Turn the tracing paper over again and place it on your sheet of paper or cardboard. Draw around the outline of the pattern, pressing hard with your pencil. The pattern will transfer onto the paper or cardboard.

3 Remove the tracing paper and make sure the line has been transferred. Go over the line with a pencil if you need to. Use scissors to cut out the template and then draw around it as shown in the project pictures.

Dinosaur template

Shadow Show
Spider template

Crocodile Tunnel
guide

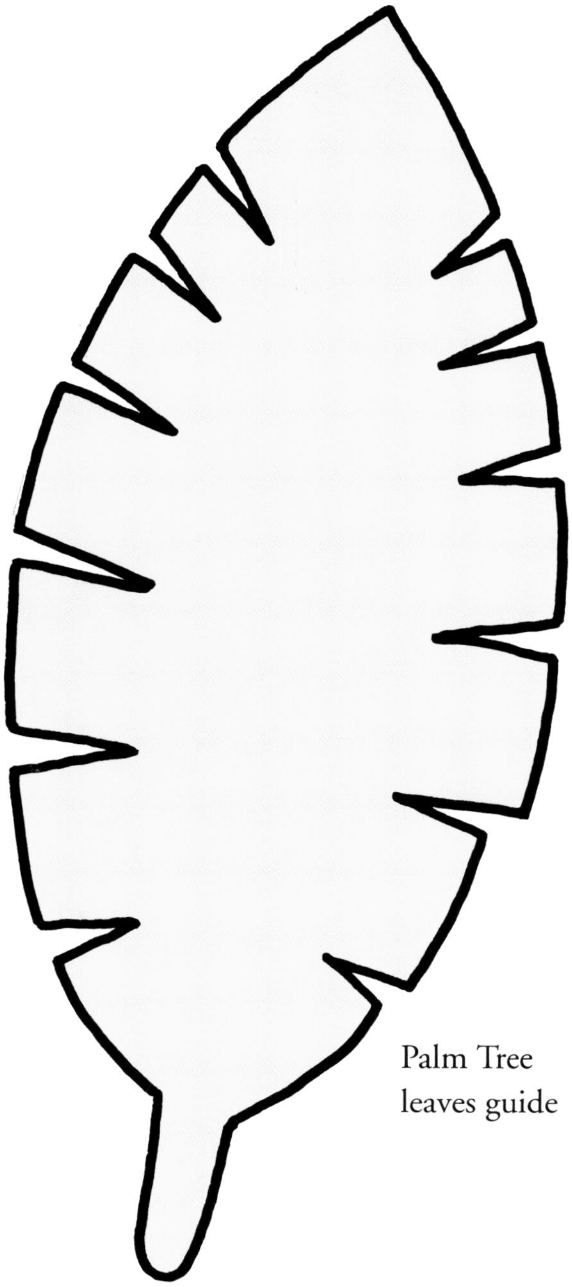

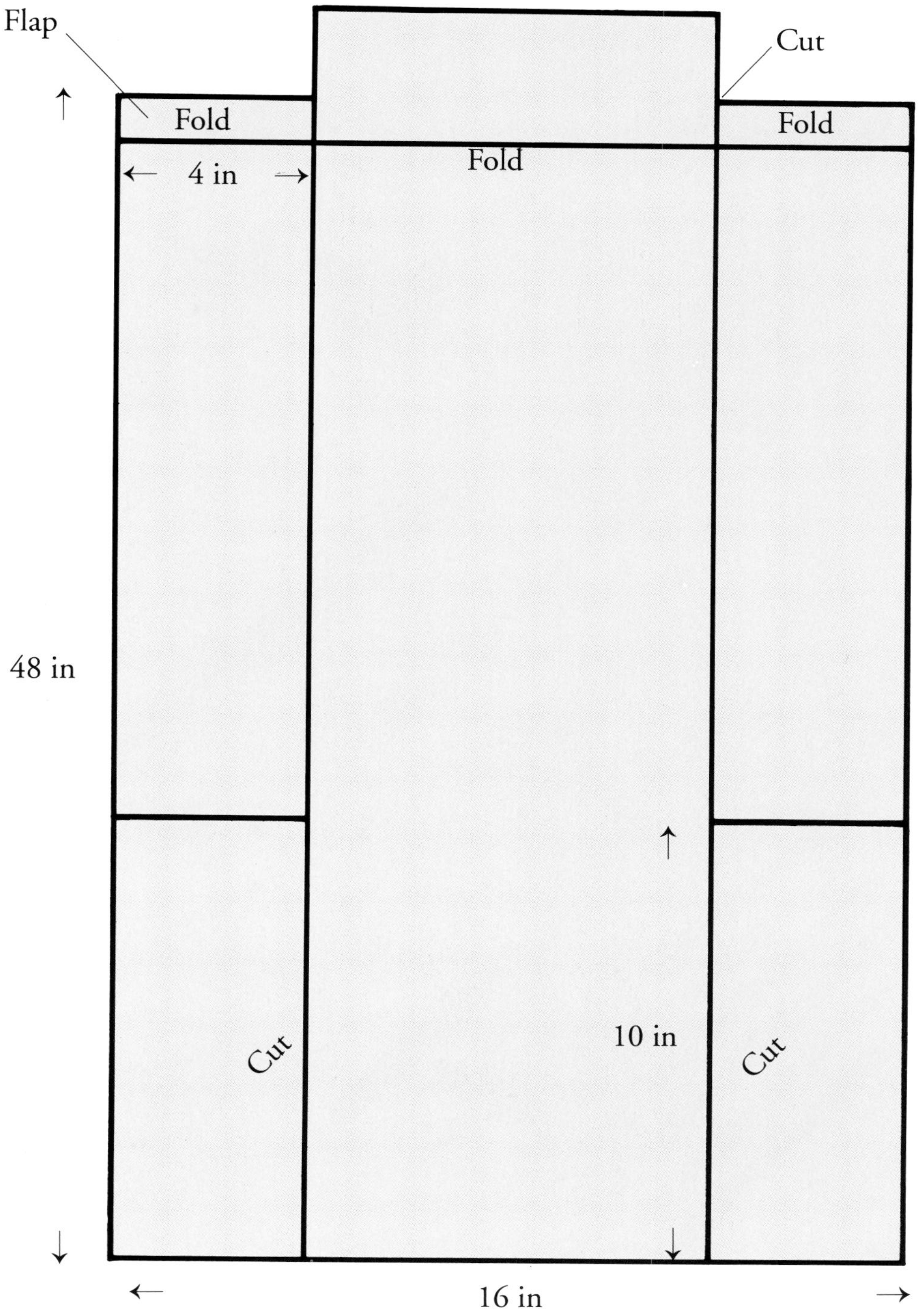

Flap

Cut

Fold

Fold

Fold

← 4 in →

48 in

10 in

Cut

Cut

Palm Tree
leaves guide

← 16 in →

Materials and Equipment

Some basic tools and pieces of equipment are used again and again in this book. A ruler, a pencil, scissors, paintbrushes and a glue brush are all essentials.

Most projects involve a fair amount of glue. The white glue most frequently used is sometimes called wood glue. This type of glue takes time to dry, but once dry it is very strong. When gluing flat paper onto a flat surface, white glue can cause the paper to wrinkle. For that sort of job a glue stick is a better choice. Remember that glue sticks dry up very quickly if you leave the lid off. Masking tape is good for holding surfaces or objects together while the glue dries.

Paint

There are many different kinds of paint. The paint used in this book is acrylic paint, which is also called poster paint.

Water jar

Finger paints

Acrylic paints

Poster paints

Ruler

Glue brush

Knife

Felt-tipped pens

Teaspoon

Brushes

Scissors

Compass

White glue and glue spreader

Pencils

Sharpener

If you need to paint a large surface, such as the crocodile tunnel, it is worth using latex paint. Latex paints are water-based. This means you have to wash your brushes and hands in water to clean them, but you have to wash the paint off immediately, before it has a chance to dry.

You can find many of the materials used in this book around your home. Cardboard boxes can be cut up into sheets of cardboard. Try to save them when you receive a package or buy shoes. Egg cartons are fantastic. In this book we have only one project using an egg carton, but they can be used to hold objects while you paint them. Yogurt containers are also very useful, not only as a project material but as holders for keeping objects still while you paint them.

Finally, whatever projects you decide to make, take care of your materials and equipment. Keep your tools in a box. Store paper flat so that it doesn't get wrinkled or torn.

Have a good party!

Tinsel

Paper plate

Egg box

Crepe paper

Colored paper

Masking tape

Glue stick

Tissue paper

Doily

Elastic

Raffia ribbon

Strong colored tape (wide)

Star stickers

Cup hook

Tacks

Strong colored tape (narrow)

Pins

Curtain ring

Tinsel pipe cleaners

Bamboo stick

Paper Chains

Paper chains are a must for every party. They are fun and easy to make. You can decorate your home by hanging them along walls and over doorways, and they look great with balloons. You may need to hang them up with tacks, so make sure you ask a grown-up for help. Amy is making some special, patterned paper chains.

Use as many bright colors as you want to. At Christmas use festive, seasonal red and green.

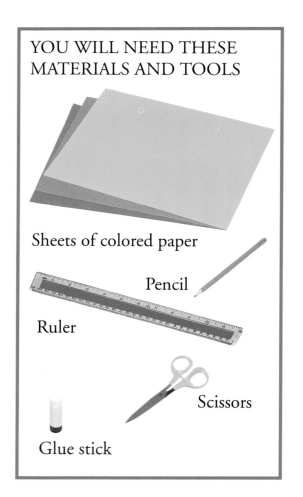

YOU WILL NEED THESE
MATERIALS AND TOOLS

Sheets of colored paper

Pencil

Ruler

Scissors

Glue stick

1 Using a pencil, draw lines lengthways down the sheets of colored paper. Draw the lines a ruler's width apart (about 1½ in).

2 Draw a line across the paper, so that each rectangle on the colored paper measures 10 in.

3 Cut out the rectangles as carefully as possible. Amy is cutting several sheets of paper together, to save time.

4 Make two piles of rectangles, with the same number in each pile. Fold all the rectangles in one pile in half. Draw a lattice pattern on them.

5 Cut out the pattern on all the rectangles in the pile. Keep the paper folded while you cut. Make sure the cuts are even.

6 Unfold your cut-out rectangle and glue it onto a plain rectangle from the other pile using a glue stick. Repeat until you have made all the colored rectangles into the links for your paper chain.

7 Stick the ends of the first link together. Put another link through the first one and stick the ends together. Repeat this with all your links.

You can make plain colored links too, to mix and match.

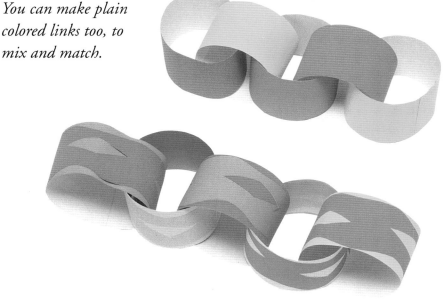

Palm Trees

Treasure Island parties make for great adventures. You and your guests can dress up as pirates and sailors. Nicholas is making some palm trees to put on the table with all the party food. An adult could help you make larger palm trees to stick in the yard or around the driveway. To make the larger trees, use larger sheets of paper or glue several sheets of paper together.

Where to put it
Put your palm trees in places where they won't easily get knocked over!

YOU WILL NEED THESE MATERIALS AND TOOLS

2 pieces of thin cardboard, or thick construction paper: one orange and one green

Tracing paper

Soft pencil

Scissors

Tape

3 wooden sticks

Sand

Strong green duct tape

Yogurt container

Aluminum foil

Strong yellow tape

1 Draw a leaf 40 cm long and 20 cm wide on green cardboard. Use the guide to help you. Cut it out. Make three leaves for each tree.

2 Roll the orange cardboard or paper into a long tube. Hold the tube firmly so it doesn't uncurl, and cut a fringe into the top edge of the roll.

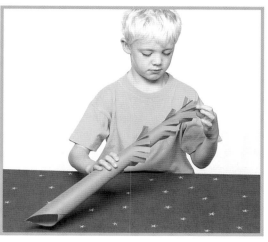

3 Still holding the tube firmly, gently pull out the inside edge of the cardboard to make the trunk of your tree.

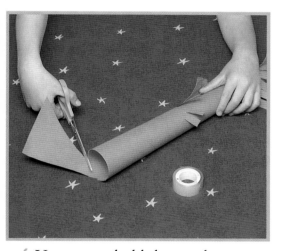

4 Use tape to hold the trunk together at the base. Trim the base, so that the trunk can stand up straight.

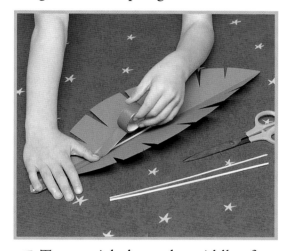

5 Tape a stick down the middle of each palm leaf, Use green tape so that it doesn't show.

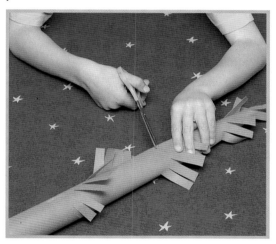

6 Cut two slits on opposite sides of the trunk, just big enough to hold the stalks of the leaves. Make the slits 4 in from the top of the trunk.

7 Slide a palm leaf into each slit. Push the third leaf into the top of the trunk and tape it in place.

8 Cover the yogurt container with aluminum foil. Use yellow tape to make stripes around it. Fill the pot with sand and push the tree into it.

"I Am Four" Badge

Deborah is making a badge to show everyone how old she will be at her birthday party. Make one for your age and wear it with your best party outfit. You could also start a collection for every birthday. Age badges make great presents, too! The badge is made from papier mâché, which is paper soaked in glue mixed with water.

Handy collecting tip
Cardboard boxes are always useful to have around for making things. If you don't have any colored paper, use pages from a magazine instead. Some of the colors are great for making flowers. Make sure you ask, before you cut up someone's magazine!

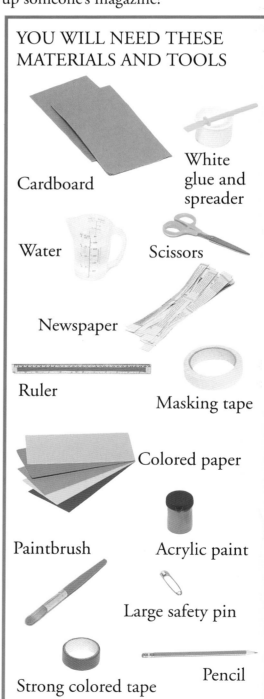

YOU WILL NEED THESE
MATERIALS AND TOOLS

Cardboard

White glue and spreader

Water

Scissors

Newspaper

Ruler

Masking tape

Colored paper

Paintbrush

Acrylic paint

Large safety pin

Strong colored tape

Pencil

1 Draw your chosen number on cardboard. Cut it out carefully and draw around it onto three more pieces of cardboard. Cut out the numbers so that you have four cardboard numbers.

2 Prepare the papier mâché by mixing equal amounts of white glue and water in a bowl. Cut newspaper into strips, and leave the strips to soak in the glue and water.

3 Meanwhile, stick the four cardboard numbers together with glue. Then wrap masking tape around them to hold them together.

4 Paint the badge with glue, using the brush, and stick on a layer of wet paper strips. Allow to dry in a warm place, and then stick on a second layer.

5 While the papier mâché is drying, cut out paper flowers from brightly colored paper. Cut out circles for the centers of the flowers.

6 Paint your badge with acrylic paint. You might need to use two layers of paint to cover the newspaper. Allow to dry.

7 Glue on the paper flowers, then glue on contrasting circles for the centers. Allow to dry.

8 Use strong colored tape to stick the non-opening side of the safety pin to the back of the badge.

Tropical Bird Mask and Wings

It's really easy and fun to make fancy costumes, whatever the theme. Brooke has made a fantastic tropical bird with wings and a beak. She is going to wear it to her Easter Parade party. Make sure the paper you use is thick enough so that it doesn't rip if you run around.

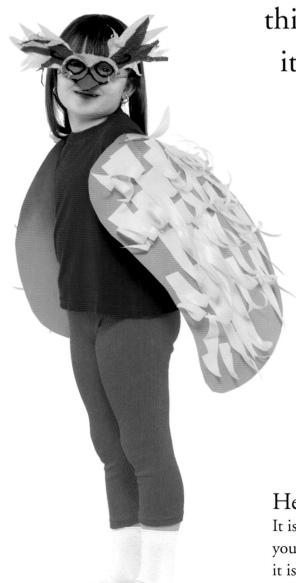

Helpful hint

It is easier if a friend or grown-up helps you fit the elastic on your mask, so that it isn't too tight or too loose. Ask an adult to pierce a hole in each side of the mask with scissors or a skewer.

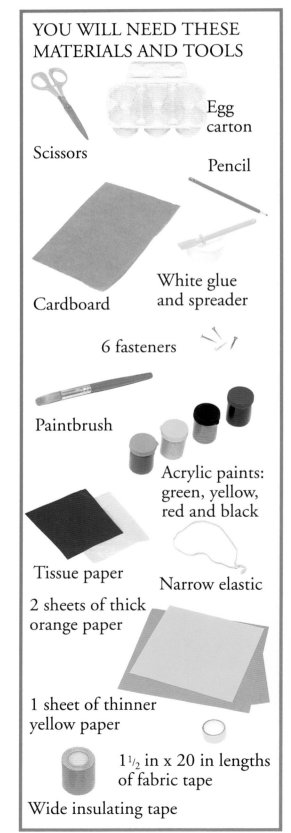

YOU WILL NEED THESE MATERIALS AND TOOLS

Scissors

Egg carton

Pencil

Cardboard

White glue and spreader

6 fasteners

Paintbrush

Acrylic paints: green, yellow, red and black

Tissue paper

Narrow elastic

2 sheets of thick orange paper

1 sheet of thinner yellow paper

$1\frac{1}{2}$ in x 20 in lengths of fabric tape

Wide insulating tape

1 Ask a grown-up to help you cut the eyes and beak out of the egg carton. Cut out two egg compartments. Cut out eyeholes.

2 Cut out big eyelashes from the cardboard. Fold and glue the ends to the eyes. Push fasteners through both layers and open out. Allow to dry.

3 Using acrylic paint, paint the eyes green, the eyelashes yellow and the beak red. Paint a black line around the eyes and the beak. Allow to dry.

4 Cut feather shapes from tissue paper and glue onto the eyelashes. Ask an adult to make holes in the sides of the mask. Thread the holes with elastic, so that it fits around your head.

5 Draw a wing shape on one of the sheets of orange paper. Make the wing as big as possible. Cut it out and draw around it onto the second orange sheet. Cut out the second wing.

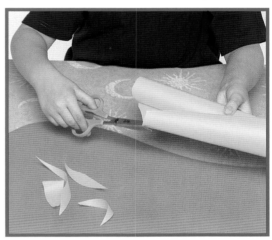

6 Roll up the piece of yellow paper and cut it into curly, feather-shaped strips. Glue these onto the orange wings.

7 Make three cuts about 3 in deep at the top of the wings so they will fit on your shoulders.

8 Overlap the paper cuts and fasten with a fastener. Use the tapes to tie around the upper arm and waist.

Christmas Tree Hat

Nicholas has made a hat to celebrate Christmas. It has a star of Bethlehem on top, just like those you find on Christmas trees. He will definitely be the star of the party. You can make other hats, too, such as a sunshine hat or a flower hat for a summer party. Make these hats the same way as the Christmas hat, but with a big sun or flower instead of a star.

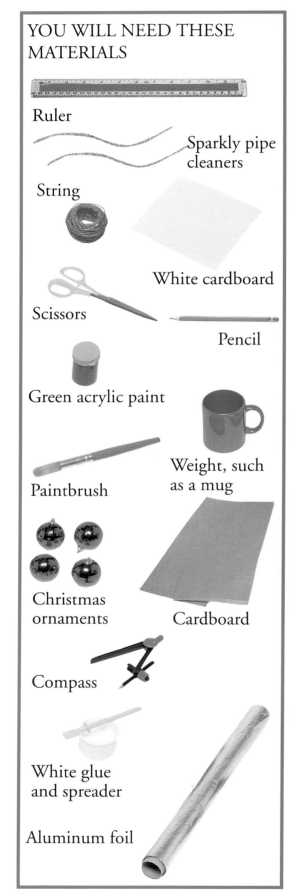

YOU WILL NEED THESE MATERIALS

Ruler

Sparkly pipe cleaners

String

White cardboard

Scissors

Pencil

Green acrylic paint

Weight, such as a mug

Paintbrush

Christmas ornaments

Cardboard

Compass

White glue and spreader

Aluminum foil

1 Measure your head with the piece of string, then add 3 in onto the length of the string.

2 Cut a piece of white cardboard the same length as the string. Draw a dotted line down the center. Draw a Christmas tree with tabs top and sides.

3 Cut out the tree shape including the tabs at the top and sides. Paint it green and allow to dry.

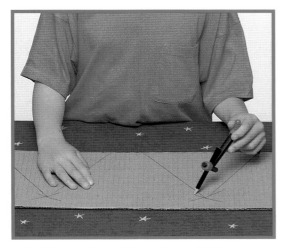

4 On a piece of cardboard, draw and cut out two triangles with 7 in sides. Draw the bottom of the triangle first, then use the compass to mark the top point.

5 Stick the two triangles together to make a star with six points. Glue aluminum foil onto the star and leave it to dry.

6 Glue the tab at the top of the tree to the back of the star. Allow to dry under a weight so the two pieces can bond together. Ask a grown-up to trim the tabs to fit.

7 Tape the side tabs together so the hat fits around your head. Allow to dry. Tape tinsel around the hat.

8 Use sparkly pipe cleaners to attach Christmas ornaments around the hat.

Treasure Chest

Amy has made a treasure chest and filled it with prizes, so that each of her guests leaves the party with a going-away present. She has wrapped all the presents in gold paper, so they look like treasure, and added bags of chocolate coins. The presents don't need to be big or expensive, just fun. She is going to hide her treasure trove until the end of the party, then everyone will play "hunt for the treasure chest." The winner gets the first pick of the prizes.

Safety tip

When making holes with a pair of scissors, always make sure the blades are closed together and that you point the tip of them away from you.

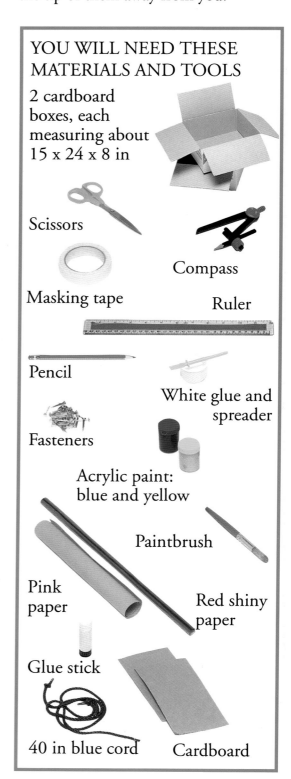

YOU WILL NEED THESE MATERIALS AND TOOLS

2 cardboard boxes, each measuring about 15 x 24 x 8 in

Scissors

Compass

Masking tape

Ruler

Pencil

White glue and spreader

Fasteners

Acrylic paint: blue and yellow

Paintbrush

Pink paper

Red shiny paper

Glue stick

40 in blue cord

Cardboard

1 Cut three of the flaps off one of the boxes, leaving one of the long flaps attached. This will be used for the lid.

2 Cut up the second box, leaving the base, one long and two short sides. Draw a semicircle on each short side.

3 Use the compass to draw the semicircles, as shown in the picture for Step 2. Cut them out.

4 Fold up the semicircles to make the sides of the lid. Place the long side of the box in the middle and hold in place with masking tape.

5 Cut a 24 in square of cardboard. Ask a grown-up to score the cardboard to help it bend. Glue it to the sides and secure with masking tape.

6 Cut the flap on the first box to make two hinges. Glue the lid onto the hinges and leave to dry. Stud with fasteners, putting glue under each pin.

7 Paint the outside of the chest with blue acrylic paint. With the glue stick, glue on yellow stripes to create a barrel effect. Add a keyhole and pink skulls and crossbones.

8 Line the chest with paper. Pierce two holes in either side of the box base. Thread cord into each and knot, then glue onto the lid. Hold in place with masking tape until dry.

Crocodile Tunnel

Susie has collected lots of big cardboard boxes to make a colorful crocodile tunnel. She and her friends can open and close the mouth as the crocodile appears to eat them up. If you want, make another animal instead: an elephant, a horse or a big snake. Another great idea is to make just a crocodile's head. Put up a tent in the garden and place the head at the entrance. You can crawl inside and sit inside your fat crocodile's stomach!

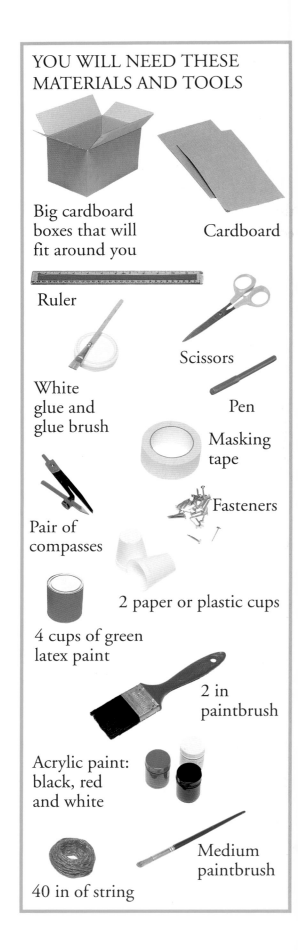

YOU WILL NEED THESE MATERIALS AND TOOLS

Big cardboard boxes that will fit around you

Cardboard

Ruler

White glue and glue brush

Scissors

Pen

Masking tape

Pair of compasses

Fasteners

2 paper or plastic cups

4 cups of green latex paint

2 in paintbrush

Acrylic paint: black, red and white

40 in of string

Medium paintbrush

1 Cut the two short top flaps of a cardboard box into triangles. Cut the two long flaps to have a straight edge 12 in long. Open up the bottom.

2 To make the snout, cut out cardboard 16 in by 48 in. Use the guide in the book to help you. Cut zigzags for teeth, and flaps as marked.

3 Cut up to the lines, and glue the corners together. Secure them with fasteners. Repeat for the other half of the croc's jaw.

4 Attach the snout to one long flap of the box you prepared in Step 1. Use glue, masking tape and fasteners.

5 Cut out two pieces of cardboard 6 in by 4 in. Use a compass to make a curve on each. Cut them out.

6 Draw around the cups. Cut out two circles with scissors, and fit the cups into the holes.

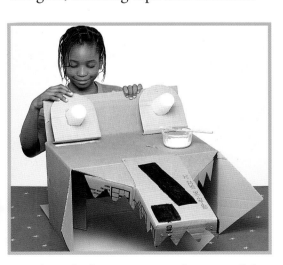

7 Attach the eyes onto the top of the head by folding the straight edge and gluing it down. Hold each eye in place at the top with a fastener.

8 Paint your crocodile head. Ask a grown-up to pierce a hole in the nose. Thread string through and tie a knot at each end. This will allow you to open and close the mouth.

For the croc's body, open up other cardboard boxes, glue the flaps, and paint.

Shadow Show Spider

Halloween is a celebration of ghosts, spiders and witches. Nicholas is making some shadow sticks to cast larger-than-life shadows. You can make a whole spooky shadow show. Hang up a white sheet and stand behind the sheet with a light behind you, or stand in front of a light and cast shadows onto the walls. You could make other shadow show shapes – the more witches, bats and toads the better.

YOU WILL NEED THESE MATERIALS AND TOOLS

Tracing paper

Soft pencil

Light-colored pencil

Black card-board

Glue stick

Scissors

Sticks

Strong black tape

24

1 Copy the spider template onto tracing paper. Scribble over the spider in light-colored pencil.

2 Turn it over, then draw around the outline with a pencil to transfer the spider onto the black cardboard.

3 Cut out your spider around the outline of the template. Be careful not to cut the legs off!

4 Cut out little strips of black cardboard to make the spider's teeth. Glue them into place.

5 Tape the stick onto the back of the spider with strong black tape. Hide the stick behind one of the spider's teeth.

Arty Party Wall

Making a fun wall is always a huge success at parties. You and your guests can draw on it, and leave messages or your names. Here Christopher has drawn a picture of the sea, but you can choose any theme. Leave lots of pens and pencils in jars next to the wall. You'll be left with a masterpiece.

Material suggestion

If you can't get hold of a large roll of colored paper, buy some shelf lining paper or simple patterned wallpaper from a hardware store.

YOU WILL NEED THESE MATERIALS AND TOOLS

Several sheets of colored paper

Scissors

Pencils in different colors

Glue stick

1 large roll of paper, approximately 40 in square

Tacks

Balloons

Strong black tape

1 Cut out long wiggly strips of green paper to make seaweed.

2 Draw the outlines of some fish onto colored paper, using light-colored pencils on dark paper. The fish should be quite large. Cut them out neatly.

3 Cut out eyes and patterns from colored paper and glue them onto your fish with a glue stick.

4 Tack or tape your large sheet of paper to the wall. Decorate the corners with balloons. Ask a grown-up to help if you are using tacks.

5 Glue on your cut-out fish and seaweed. Arrange them so that they look nice, but leave room for other drawings too.

6 Draw on lots of creatures and write messages with your friends.

Gone Fishin'

Houw is making a fishing game. Each player has to hook up as many floating fish as possible when the music is on. The player who catches the most fish wins. This game is best played in the garden or kitchen, as it's easy to splash lots of water around.

Houw has used bowls to make his fish ponds, but small plastic wading pools are great too.

Material note
The number of rods and bottles will depend on how many friends want to play. Make sure there are about three fish bottles per player.

YOU WILL NEED THESE
MATERIALS AND TOOLS

10–20 small plastic drinks bottles with twist-off tops

Paintbrush

Acrylic paint

White glue and glue spreader

String

10–20 curtain rings

Scissors

5 bamboo sticks

Blue food coloring

Strong colored tape

5 plastic-coated screw-in cup hooks

Tissue paper

2 or 3 bowls

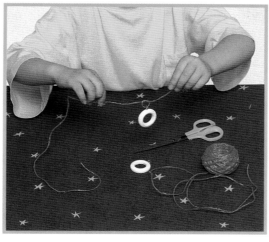

1 Wash the bottles and soak off the labels. Allow to dry, then screw the lids back on. Paint fish shapes onto the bottles. Mix glue into your paint so that it sticks to the plastic.

2 Cut string into lengths of 18 in. Tie the end of each piece of string onto the hook in a curtain ring. Do this with as many curtain rings as there are bottles.

3 Tie the string onto the bottles with a double knot so that the curtain ring dangles a bit.

4 To make the paint waterproof, mix a varnish of three parts glue to one part water. Apply two coats to the painted fish bottles. Allow the glue to dry between coats.

5 To make the fishing rods, decorate the bamboo sticks with bands of colored tape,

6 Screw a cup hook firmly into the end of the rod.

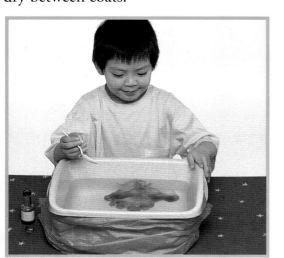

7 Wrap tissue paper around the bowls. Add food coloring to the water.

Coconut Toss

You don't need coconuts to make a Coconut Toss. Gaby is making her own version of a game you sometimes find at carnivals. Her game has lots of funny faces. To play, set your coconuts on a table. Mark a line at a distance in front of the table where the players have to stand. Then try and knock the faces out of the pots by tossing the little ball. Make sure the pots are weighted down and tied to the table. Have as many as you need – eight is a good number.

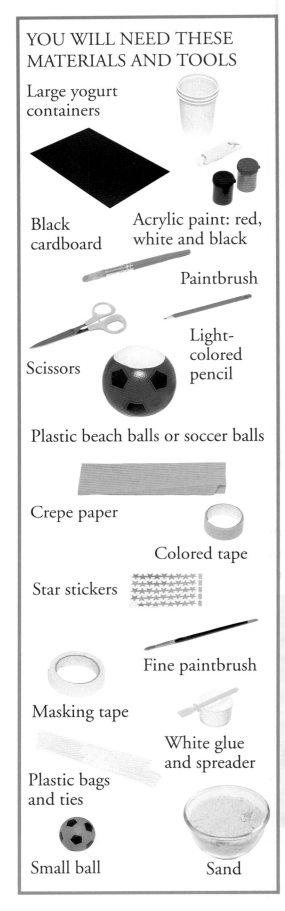

YOU WILL NEED THESE MATERIALS AND TOOLS

Large yogurt containers

Black cardboard

Acrylic paint: red, white and black

Paintbrush

Scissors

Light-colored pencil

Plastic beach balls or soccer balls

Crepe paper

Colored tape

Star stickers

Fine paintbrush

Masking tape

White glue and spreader

Plastic bags and ties

Small ball

Sand

1 Paint the sides of the yogurt containers white. Allow to dry.

2 Draw a black mustache on black cardboard with a light-colored pencil and cut it out.

3 Paint a white circle onto your ball and leave it to dry. It is easier if you balance the ball on a yogurt container so it doesn't roll around.

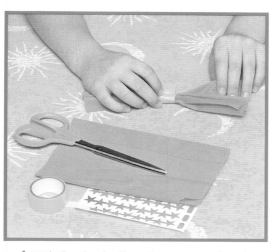

4 While the ball is drying, make the bow tie. Cut crepe paper so that it measures 6 in by 4 in. Fold it several times. Tie the middle with a piece of tape and stick on some stars.

5 Paint a face onto the ball using a fine brush and black and red acrylic paints.

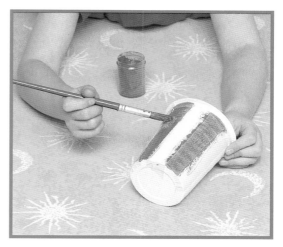

6 Once the paint on the yogurt containers is dry, stick strips of masking tape on them, leaving 1 in gaps. Paint the gaps with red acrylic paint and leave to dry.

7 Stick the mustache and bow tie onto the ball. Peel the masking tape off the yogurt containers.

8 Fill a plastic bag with sand and twist a tie around the top. Place it in the pot and put the ball on top.

Apple Bobbing

Apple bobbing is a game traditionally played at Halloween, but is great to play at parties throughout the year. You have to get the apples out of the bowl without using your hands, as Susie and Patty are trying to do! It's alot of fun, but can be wet and messy, so wear a raincoat or plastic apron. It's also a good idea to place the bowl on a table in the kitchen. Decorate the bowl to suit your theme. Happy bobbing!

Finger paint
You can buy paint especially for finger painting, but acrylic paint is also fine. Have a cloth handy for cleaning up, as it can get very messy.

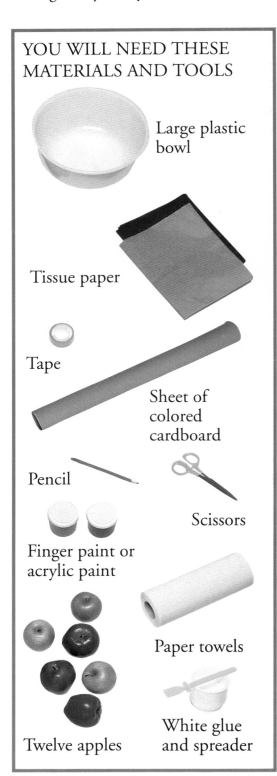

YOU WILL NEED THESE MATERIALS AND TOOLS

Large plastic bowl

Tissue paper

Tape

Sheet of colored cardboard

Pencil

Scissors

Finger paint or acrylic paint

Paper towels

Twelve apples

White glue and spreader

1 To decorate the bowl, attach a folded stack of tissue paper just under the edge of the bowl with tape. Then gather the paper to fit around the bottom and tape it down. Do this with three more wads of tissue paper.

2 Draw an apple shape onto the cardboard. Remember to use a pencil that will show up.

3 Cut the apple shape out, then draw around it to make three more apples. Cut them out, too.

4 Finger-paint the apples with red dots. Keep a paper towel handy to wipe your fingers on, and wash your hands when you have finished.

5 Stick each apple onto the tissue paper with glue. Allow to dry.

6 Put the bowl on a table or the floor and ask a grown-up to fill the bowl with water and the apples.

Easter Egg Hunt

An Easter party is the perfect excuse for an egg hunt. Hide your decorated eggs around the house or in the yard for all your friends to find. David is turning eggs into Easter rabbits. Count your guests and then decorate the same number of eggs. Remember to make one for yourself, too! Some people blow the eggs out of their shells, but it is easier to boil them – as long as you don't keep them too long.

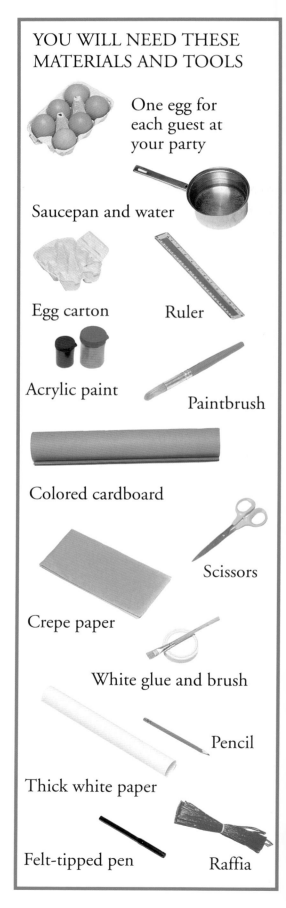

YOU WILL NEED THESE MATERIALS AND TOOLS

One egg for each guest at your party

Saucepan and water

Egg carton

Ruler

Acrylic paint

Paintbrush

Colored cardboard

Scissors

Crepe paper

White glue and brush

Pencil

Thick white paper

Felt-tipped pen

Raffia

34

1 Ask a grown-up to put the eggs into cold water. Bring the water to a boil, and boil the eggs for 10 minutes. Rinse the eggs in cold water to cool them. Then put them back in the carton to dry.

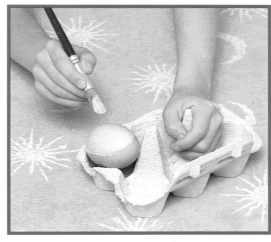

2 Once the eggs have dried, paint an oval on one side of each to make the rabbit face. Allow the paint to dry.

3 Cut out rabbit ears from the colored cardboard, 2½ in long and 1 in at the widest point. Cut smaller pieces of crepe paper and glue them onto the ears.

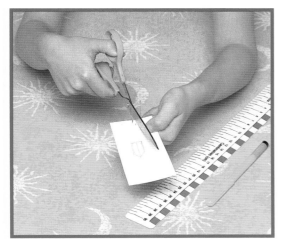

4 Draw the teeth on thick white paper (they should be ¾ in by ½ in). Cut them out.

5 Cut six raffia whiskers for each egg. They should be 2 in long.

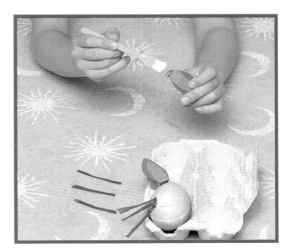

6 Glue the ears, whiskers and teeth onto the eggs. To attach the ears, fold a little part of the cardboard under, and glue that onto the egg. Leave to dry in the egg carton.

7 Draw on the eyes and nose in felt-tipped pen to make a cheerful Easter bunny.

Marzipan Dinosaur Cake

Marzipan is the delicious almond paste you find molded into shapes. You can buy marzipan from any supermarket, and it's easy to color it with food dye. Decorate a cake for yourself, for someone in your family or for a friend. Before you roll out the marzipan, wash your hands.

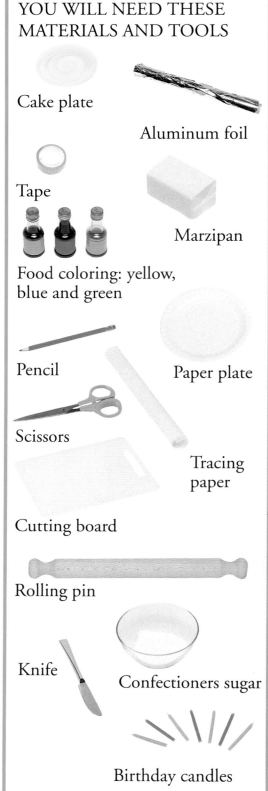

YOU WILL NEED THESE MATERIALS AND TOOLS

Cake plate

Aluminum foil

Tape

Marzipan

Food coloring: yellow, blue and green

Pencil

Paper plate

Scissors

Tracing paper

Cutting board

Rolling pin

Knife

Confectioners sugar

Birthday candles

36

1 Cover the plate with aluminum foil and use a little tape on the back to hold it.

2 Add food coloring to the marzipan, a couple of drops at a time. Knead it in thoroughly.

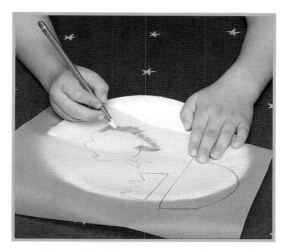

3 Trace the dinosaur template and transfer it onto the paper plate, using a soft pencil.

4 Cut out the dinosaur and the other shapes.

5 Roll out the marzipan until it is ½ in thick. Sprinkle confectioners sugar onto the rolling pin and surface to prevent the marzipan from sticking.

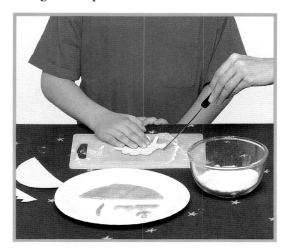

6 Ask a grown-up to cut out the marzipan with a knife, using your cardboard cut-outs as a guide.

7 Put the cake onto the plate covered in aluminum foil and carefully place the marzipan on the cake. You can help the shapes stay in place by dabbing water underneath them.

8 Push the candles into the cake. Light the candles, and it's time to sing "Happy Birthday!"

Funny Faces Fairy Cakes

These are cakes you can either decorate before your guests arrive, or make into a game at the party. Lay out all the materials and see which guest can make the silliest face or the most imaginative object out of the cakes. Anne and Gaby have made funny faces with crazy hairstyles.

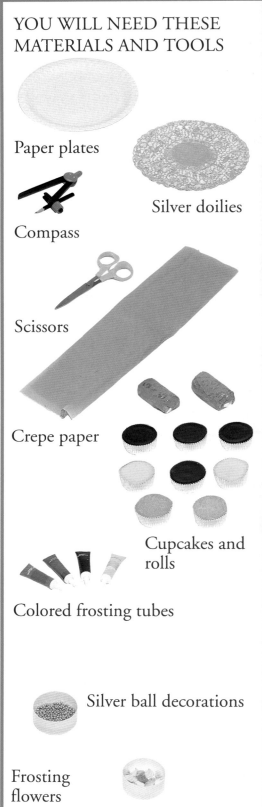

YOU WILL NEED THESE MATERIALS AND TOOLS

Paper plates

Silver doilies

Compass

Scissors

Crepe paper

Cupcakes and rolls

Colored frosting tubes

Silver ball decorations

Frosting flowers

1 Put a silver doily on a paper plate. Using a compass, draw a slightly smaller circle on crepe paper and cut it out. Place it on top of the doily.

2 Place a cup cake and a roll on the plate. These will be the head and body.

3 Squeezing the frosting tubes gently, pipe on the mouth, eyes and nose, using different colors.

4 Put silver balls on the eyes to make them sparkle.

5 To make the jacket, frost on stripes and buttons. Add frosting flower decorations and silver balls.

6 Add some curly hair with a different color frosting.

7 Add arms, hands and a skirt by piping colored frosting straight onto the pink paper. Add some frosting flowers for the feet and your work of art is ready to eat!

"Seven Today" Sandwiches

Patty loves cheese sandwiches, and wanted to make them special for her party. She is celebrating her seventh birthday and has made sandwiches in the shape of her new age. The lettuce and radishes are not only healthy and decorative, but also delicious. She has split the number seven sandwiches into two parts so they are easy to eat, bite by bite!

Clean cook alert

Don't forget to wash your hands before you start cooking. And be careful when you're using a knife.

YOU WILL NEED THESE MATERIALS AND TOOLS

Paper napkins

Brown bread

Lettuce

Radishes

Large plate

Knife

Cheese

Cutting board

40

1 Cut the two loose edges of the napkin into a zigzag pattern.

2 Unfold the napkin and put it on a plate that's big enough.

3 Place two pieces of bread on top of each other and cut off the crusts.

4 Cut a triangle off of one corner of the bread. Ask a grown-up to help you do this.

5 Now cut a small triangle from the other side, leaving you with a number seven shape. Cut the seven in two parts through the corner.

6 Arrange the bottoms of the sandwiches on the plate, and fill with slices of cheese cut to the right shape. Garnish the spaces with lettuce.

7 Slice the radishes carefully and use them to decorate the tops of the sandwiches.

8 Ask your guests to guess your age when you serve your sandwiches!

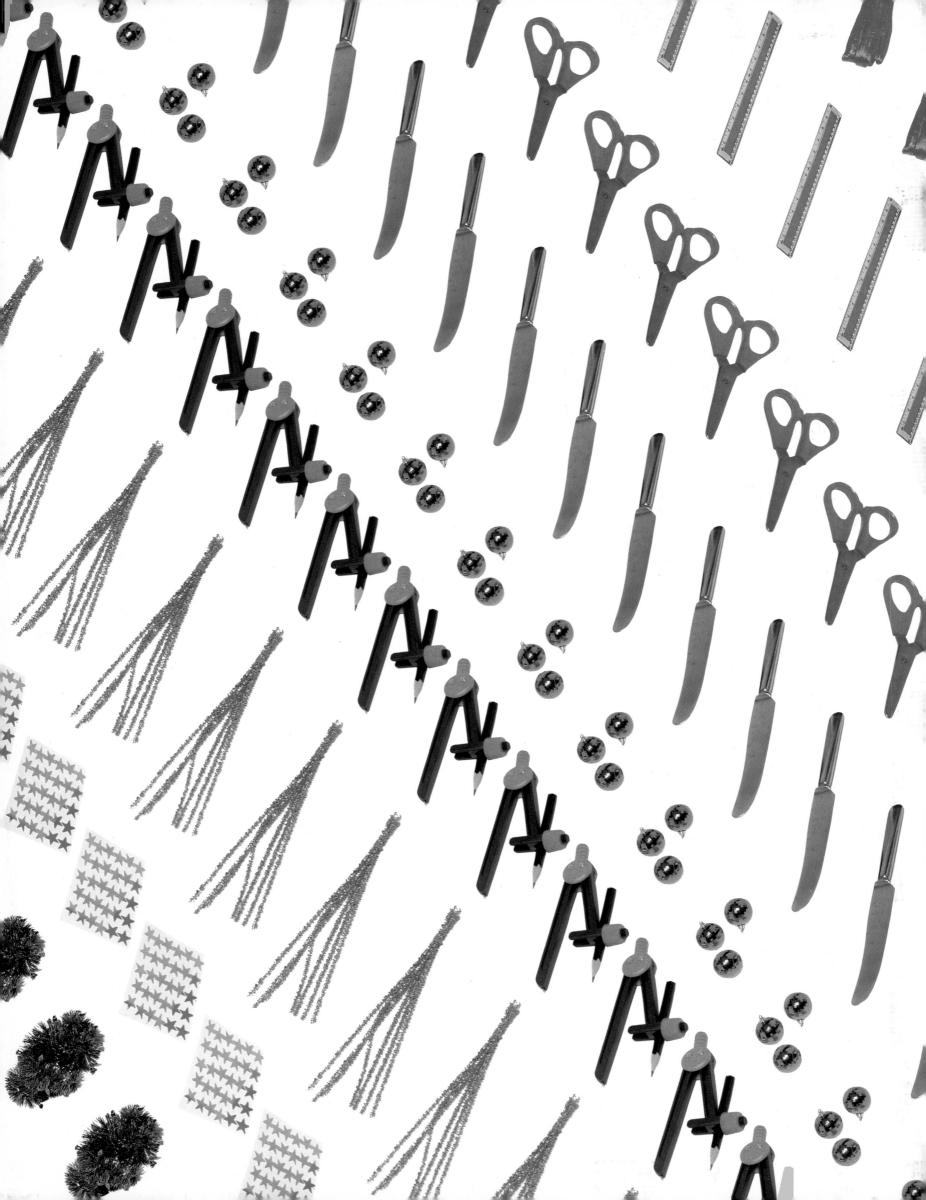